Bercée au vent du Nord

Liliane Wouters

Rocking to the North Wind

translated from the French by

Anne-Marie Glasheen

Poetry Europe Series No. 10

DEDALUS

The Dedalus Press
24 The Heath
Cypress Downs
Dublin 6 W
Ireland

ISBN 1 901233 57 X

Dedalus Press books are represented and distributed in the
U.S.A. and Canada by Dufour Editions Ltd., P.O. Box 7,
Chester Springs, Pennsylvania 19425
and in the UK by Central Books, 99 Wallis Road, London
E9 5LN

The Dedalus Press receives financial assistance from
An Chomhairle Ealaíon, The Arts Council, Ireland.

Printed in Ireland by Colour Books Ltd., Dublin

Contents

The Dedalus Press

Rocking to the North Wind

Liliane Wouters

Liliane Wouters was born into a humble family in Ixelles, Brussels, on — 'a snowy day' — February 5, 1930. At home she spoke Flemish, at school French. An ideal person to represent the mingling of the two main cultures that make Belgium. During the occupation her friends starred in the plays she wrote. In 1944 she started her training to be a teacher. She taught for thirty years in a convent in Brussels until she took early retirement in 1980. She also wrote poetry.

Then one day she sent a bundle of poems to the poet Roger Bodart. He was very encouraging, helped her correct them, and in 1954, her first collection, *La marche forcée*, was published. These early poems revealed an extraordinary understanding of and facility with words, and a life-force that was far from being filled with optimism. Ever present is the conflict between good and evil, as a young woman struggles against the opposing extremes to which she is drawn. We witness the crisis of faith, 'I have torn up my Bible and spat on the Cross,' and share the ensuing emptiness. Not only does she identify her despair, she identifies with it. She picks away at it the way a child picks at a scab only to discover that he who would die must first be born. Her capacity to suffer was a gift from the bad fairy bestowed at birth. Writing poetry would be a form of exorcism.

The title, *La marche forcée* (Forced March) introduces the sense of disillusionment and the nature of the demands that were to permeate her work, as well as the tensions that took so long to subside. What is so astonishing about this first collection is that she had intuitively sown the seeds of all her questions and unveiled a personality in all its sincerity. Her sense of the present, of history and its relation with the present; her sense of eternity, her patience, her impatience, her search for love, her quest for a crusade worth dying for, her burying of the Good Lord. In fifty years of writing, these are the themes to which Liliane Wouters has constantly returned.

The collection was an instant success. In Paris she was awarded the Prix de la Nuit de poésie by a panel of judges that included Aragon, Audiberti, Auric, Cocteau, Gilson, Reverdy and Seghers. Louis Aragon praised her 'technique and mastery of French versification.' Praise indeed from a Marxist, given the nature of the themes: faith, God, the Promised Land and the Bible. She would return to geographical areas of the Bible in a later work, *Journal du scribe*.

Published in 1960, *Le bois sec* was a significant leap forward in her exploration of inner conflicts and her sense of isolation. Hailed by René Lacôte as 'the most truly French poet of her generation', this is the book of a thirty-year-old woman only too aware of the undeniable and inevitable: he who would live must die. The time had come to choose between the principal opposing forces that were tearing her apart. Reviewing the collection, Alain Bosquet described her as being 'reduced to a majestic distress, tortured but stoical, caught between earthly temptations and an inaccessible mysticism'. With, he concluded, 'God under her skin and the devil in her body'.

It is in *Le gel* that she at last reaches the icy solitude of what she refers to as le séjour sans larmes (the tearless time). Gone is the soul's battling with its faith, what we have is the poet wholly able to express what no longer has boundaries or limits. There is solitude but no dereliction, rather the poet is fascinated by this frozen inner castle. Gone is the fire and emotion, the poet abandons herself to rigorous mental introspection, offers herself to the ice, to the cold's 'precious scalpel' — ready to sacrifice everything so that the words that burn can be uttered. She admits that to achieve this she had to cut herself off from what had been an essential part of her: her automatic connecting of the act of writing poetry with what can only be termed 'the sacred'.

In 1983, seventeen years later, during which time she concentrated on translations, anthologies and her dramatic writings, there was a return to poetry with the publication of the collection *L'aloès*, although the poem that bears that title first appeared at the end of *Le gel*. While nothing blooms in ice, the bitter aloe, which grows in arid soil, flowers just once every hundred years. And while *Lieu commun* opens with the funeral of a poet, *Testament* is devoted 'to the child I never had'. She bequeaths to this imaginary foetus, her strengths and weaknesses, her hopes and disappointments, all that she intuited and all that she was blind to.

Journal du scribe first came out, in a limited edition, in 1986. It is a long meditation where scribe and poet are fused, where, when the scribe says 'I', he is speaking across the centuries of and for himself and the poet. In his journeyings through Egyptian and Biblical landscapes recording history, the solitary scribe soliloquises non-stop, on the subject of men and the gods, the living and the dead, but above all himself. The scribe's tireless peregrinations symbolise the mental wanderings of his double, the poet.

Le billet de Pascal opens with the poet driving her car between Brussels and Charleroi, radio on in the background. Various news items and a kind of Desert Island Discs take her back to the past, via the philosopher, as she meditates on her birth, the deaths of an aunt and her grandmother, as she continues with her delving and questioning, picking away at present reality and past events in her pursuit of truth and understanding. Again the images of fire and ashes, the concerns with mortality and immortality: 'I am, I was not. I am, will no longer be'. From *Trois tombeaux* comes a homage to friend and poet, Françoise Delcarte. The funeral occasionally intrudes on her thoughts on a tree, an individual, a life, and the human condition in general. Again, the poet is never in one place, in one time. Her spiritual quest has continued throughout her life, but while she has travelled through time and back and all over the globe in her oeuvre, it is always to Belgium that she returns. In the touching and occasionally satirical *Grise Belgique* she paints a critical — but humorous and tender — picture of the country that gave her life.

Liliane Wouters is undoubtedly Belgium's greatest living poet. But we should not forget her literary output as an author of anthologies, translator and playwright. Her devotion to Belgium is unquestionable, given the time and energy she has put into compiling anthologies that encompass her country's poetry — past and present. Four volumes of *La Poésie francophone de Belgique* co-edited with Alain Bosquet, and *Le siècle des femmes* co-edited with Yves Namur are just two examples. Her translations of poetry have been widely published and her adaptations for the stage have also appeared on television. Her dramatic works often broach the same themes as her poetry, if not poetry itself. *Vies et morts de Mademoiselle Shakespeare* ends with a reflection on poetry, 'What are poets for Nemesis?', 'I've already told you, nothing'. It's a question of taking first one step, then another, and so on and so forth, all your life 'to find out what life is all about'. 'The world revolved before us, and it will continue to revolve after us, but while we are here, what a difference it makes!'

Wouters remains a great lyric poet. Jean Tordeur (to whom I am greatly indebted for his perspicacious preface to *Tous les chemins conduisent à la mer*) was right to point out that she is probably one of the last proponents of a form of poetry that has been around for five centuries. In her rhymes, her rhythms, her phrasing, we find things that have disappeared, that are disappearing. Through the lyricism we are shown the emotions that precede reflection. Tears and laughter abound, and there is dancing in Breughelian scenes of jubilation and reconciliation.

10

Jean Tordeur makes the point that it is tempting to see her as having created her identity as a writer and of having used faith as cement in the construction. However, the questioning, the offering and sharing of concerns with the self are there right from the start, and there is nothing manufactured about them. This self-absorption is as evident in her early as in her later I-have-free-will work. For example, while serenity might not be the order of the day in *L'aloès* and *Journal du scribe*, there is a sense of liberation, a less anxious feel to the writing. Even detached from religion, passion — though painful — is very much in evidence, and the long meditation on time swings from the present moment to the desire for eternity (between death that rots the body and paradise as a destiny) and the question of love is only partially and temporarily answered. A lifetime spent searching out the truth: progress is dependent on self-knowledge, on mastering a body, a voice. 'I am the secretary of the party of men'. And 'I name, therefore I am'. If the answers were discovered, if serenity found, it would probably be the end of a brilliant writing career.

Prolific poet, distinguished writer. Much of her poetry and theatrical work has been translated and performed abroad. Her poetry appears in languages as diverse as German and Chinese. She has won numerous prizes, among them the Prix Montaigne de la Fondation Frederic von Schiller. In 1985 she was elected to the Académie royale de langue et de littérature françaises de Belgique. She is also a member of the Académie européenne de poésie. But this year, 2000 saw Liliane Wouters receive the most prestigious literary honour to be awarded by the French-speaking community of Belgium — the -Prix quinquennal de Littérature' — a prize that crowns her career, a lifelong achievement award given for the whole body of her work.

Anne-Marie Glasheen
London, March 2001

11

Anne-Marie Glasheen, née Poncelet, was born in 1945 of an English mother and Belgian father and spent the first six years of her life in Liège, Belgium. In 1969, she graduated from Lancaster University with a degree in French and English and began life as a literary translator in 1978.

Her translations include two collections of plays by contemporary Belgian playwrights, some of which have been performed at the Brighton and Edinburgh Festivals, as well as in London, Northern Ireland and the United States; novels; poetry; art history books and most recently, Laure Adler's biography of Marguerite Duras. She writes poetry in English and French and has published in Belgium, France, Germany, Ireland, Luxembourg and the U.K. Some of her poetry is currently being set to music.

Author of numerous articles, lecturer, broadcaster, performer, in 1994 she founded and co-ordinated *MUZE,* an exchange programme for European women writers. She is a member of the English Centre of International P.E.N., and a past Chair of the Translators Association. In 1998 she was awarded the literary translation prize by the Communauté française de Belgique.

Bercée au vent du Nord

Rocking to the North Wind

NAISSANCE DU POÈME

Mon corps s'écartera pour le laisser jaillir :
　　Après neuf mois de peine,
La mère voit soudain son ventre tressaillir
　　Pour la douleur prochaine.

O souffle ! c'est l'effort de mon fragile enfant
　　Qui lutte pour son être.
Me déchirant pour lui, je l'aide et je défends
　　Son faible corps à naître.

Sans forme ni couleur, il m'a déjà tout pris.
　　C'est moi qui le modèle
En lui prêtant mon corps, et mon sang le nourrit.
　　Croissant, il m'écartèle.

Dans un demi-sommeil on me l'arrache enfin.
　　Je trouve son visage :
Le même que j'ai vu tracé par le burin
　　Depuis le fond des âges.

Mon double, mon écho, poème en devenir,
　　Avec ta voix étrange,
Serais-tu pas le dieu qu'un soir pour m'endormir
　　Me promettait un ange ?

BIRTH OF THE POEM

My body will split to allow it to emerge.
    After nine months of striving,
The mother suddenly sees her abdomen shudder
    At the impending pain.

O breath! It is the straining of my fragile child
    As it struggles to exist.
Ripping myself for him, I help him and fight for
    His feeble body to be born.

Shapeless and colourless, already he has drained me.
    It is I that mould him
By lending him my body, and my blood feeds him.
    Growing, he tears me apart.

In half-sleep, they pluck him from me at last.
    I discover his face,
The same I have seen drawn by the chisel
    Since the beginning of time.

My double, my echo, poem in the making,
    With your strange voice,
Are you not the god that one night, to get me to sleep,
    Promised me an angel?

CHANT CRUEL

J'ai déchiré ma Bible et craché sur la Croix.
      J'ai fait le tour du monde.
J'ai vu me contempler de leur grand oeil narquois
      le Sphinx et la Joconde.

Le bien qu'on me promet, c'est d'un jour m'allonger
      sur un lit d'herbe courte.
De quoi suis-je donc fait ? Le souffle est trop léger
      et l'argile trop lourde.

Moi qui voudrais la lune et le Pérou en plus
      je n'aurai sur ma bouche
qu'un baiser du malheur, qui m'a toujours élu
      pour partager sa couche.

Mon flanc contre le sien et le glaive entre nous,
      pour conjurer ses charmes
quand il me presserait des lèvres aux genoux
      je n'ôterai point l'arme.

Trop fier pour être heureux, je ne connaîtrai pas
      la volupté modeste
d'aller avec les chiens vers la fin du repas
      pour implorer les restes.

Je ne recevrai rien puisque j'espère tout.
      Et si j'avais la lune
Il me faudrait encore un morceau de Pérou
      pour croire à ma fortune.

CRUEL SONG

I have torn up my Bible and spat on the Cross.
    I have been round the world.
I have seen stare at me the huge mocking eyes
    of the Sphinx and the Mona Lisa.

The reward I am promised, is that I shall one day lie
    on a bed of cropped grass.
What then am I made of? The breath is too light
    and the clay too heavy.

I who would ask for the moon and Peru besides
    shall have on my mouth
but a kiss from misfortune, who has always picked me
    to share his bed.

My thigh against his and the sword between us,
    to ward off his charms
when he presses me from lips to knees
    I shall not remove the weapon.

Too proud to be happy, I shall never know
    the modest voluptuousness
of going with the dogs at the end of the meal
    to beg for scraps.

I shall be given nothing since I want everything.
    And if I had the moon
I would still need a piece of Peru
    to believe in my good fortune.

Les pauvres ont de quoi se mettre sous la dent,
    de quoi remplir leur vie.
Ils ont de quoi manger, juste assez, cependant
    leur faim est assouvie.

Seigneur, si devant toi je vaux le lis des champs
    ou la colombe grise,
pardonne à la fierté cruelle de mon chant.
    Je ne l'ai point apprise.

The poor have something to put in their mouths,
     something to fill their lives.
They have something to eat, just enough, still
     their hunger is assuaged.

Lord, if to you I am worth the lilies of the field
     or the grey dove,
forgive the cruel pride of my song.
     It was not learned.

Naître pour mourir

Mort, chaque nuit tu t'allonges
Auprès de moi. Je te sens
Dans mon somme, dans mes songes,
Dans la crainte de mon sang.

Toi, le fruit de toute peine,
La fin de chaque séjour.
Je m'éveille à ton haleine.
Je te vois avant le jour.

Naître pour mourir. Qui suis-je ?
Quel crime pèse sur moi ?
Les promesses de ma tige
Ne sont que vent sous tes doigts.

Et vent les jours qui me restent.
L'un d'eux sera le dernier.
Tous ces rêves, tous ces gestes
En un moment reniés.

Frères, sauvez-moi. Je coule.
Iles de mon archipel,
Au secours ! Mais de la foule
Nul ne sort à mon appel.

Rien à faire. Porte close.
Dehors seul le bruit des rats.
Il faut attendre la chose.
Dieu sait quand elle viendra.

Born To Die

Death, each night you lie
Beside me. I feel you
In my sleep, in my dreams,
In the dread of my blood.

You, the fruit of all grief,
The end of each visit.
I wake to your breath,
See you before daybreak.

Born to die. Who am I?
What crime bears down on me?
The promises of my stock
Are but wind in your fingers.

Wind too are the days left me,
One of which will be my last.
All those dreams, all those actions
Brought together in a flash.

Brothers, save me. I'm drowning.
Isles of my archipelago,
Help! But from the crowd
None responds to my call.

Nothing to be done. Door shut.
Outside just the sound of rats.
All we can do is wait for it.
God knows when it will come.

Est-ce un rêve ? Est-ce une farce ?
A quoi jouons-nous ici ?
Ici où tant de comparses
Dansent trois tours puis merci.

Merci. Quelqu'n vous empoigne,
Vous écarte sans retour.
L'un de mes amis s'éloigne.
Bientôt ce sera mon tour.

Faut-il vraiment que l'on meure ?
Hier, une voix chantait :
'Les jours s'en vont, je demeure.'
Aujourd'hui, la voix se tait.

Pierre, Jean, François, Guillaume,
Vos refrains vivent encor.
Mais hélas, dans quel royaume
Vous promenez-vous sans corps ?

François, Jean, Guillaume, Pierre,
Ils ne nous entendent plus.
Comment sans yeux ni paupières
Répondraient-ils aux saluts ?

Tombe la prochaine neige
Sur la cendre de leurs mains.
C'est pourtant au même piège
Que vont tous nos lendemains.

Is it a dream? Is it a joke?
What are we doing here?
Here where all these extras
Go round and round then thank you.

Thank you. Someone grabs you,
Removes you for good.
A friend disappears.
My turn will come soon.

Do we really have to die?
Yesterday, a voice sang,
'The days go by, I stay.'
Today, the voice is silent.

Pierre, Jean, François, Guillaume.
Your refrains live on.
But alas, in which kingdom
Bodiless do you roam?

François, Jean, Guillaume, Pierre.
They can no longer hear us.
Eyeless and lidless, how
Can they respond to greetings?

Though the next snows will fall
On the ashes of their hands.
It will be into the same trap
That all our tomorrows will go

Un peu plus, un peu moins vite.
Ah ! ne tournons pas autour.
Encore une fois s'évitent
Nos regards. A qui le tour ?

Allez. La porte est bien close.
On est fait comme des rats.
Il faut attendre la chose
Et Dieu sait qu'elle viendra.

A bit more, a bit less fast.
Ah! We mustn't hang around.
Our eyes once again
Cannot meet. Whose turn is it?

Go on. The door is shut tight.
We are made like rats.
All we can do is wait for it.
And God knows it will come.

PLEINS POUVOIRS

1

Pleins pouvoirs. De mes hauteurs,
Je contemple cet espace
Chaotique. Spectateur
D'un univers que dépasse
Le dieu captif en mon corps,
Je connais, voluptueuse,
Ma solitude, l'accord
De mon être aux nébuleuses.
Étrangère en ce décor
De rocs, de mers et de feuilles,
J'inscris ma naissance dans
L'inconnu.
                    Que tu le veuilles
Ou non, je plante les dents
Au coeur de l'esprit, dévore
L'invisible. Nul matin
Terrestre n'offre l'aurore
De l'horizon où j'atteins
Mon zénith.
                    Enfin j'habite
Quelque part, je vois rouler
Le fleuve humain, mon orbite
Ne le frôle plus. Foulez
L'herbe natale, coulez
Des jours brefs, faune mortelle,
Pourrissante flore. J'ai
Pleins pouvoirs.
                    Votre tutelle
Est un fardeau si léger.

FULL POWERS

1

Full powers. From these heights
I survey this chaotic
Space. Spectator
Of a universe transcended
By the captive god in my body,
I know, voluptuous,
My solitude, the harmony
Between my being and the nebulae.
A stranger in this setting
Of rocks, of seas and of leaves,
I register my birth in
The unknown.
                              Whether you like it
Or no, I plant teeth
At the heart of the spirit, devour
The invisible. No morning
On earth displays the dawn
Of the horizon where I reach
My zenith.
                              At last I live
Somewhere, I see surge
The stream of humanity, my orbit
No longer touches it. Flatten
The native grass, scuttle
Brief days, mortal fauna
Rotting flora, I have
Full powers.
                              Your charge
Is so light a burden.

2

Le peuple aux altitudes suffoquant
Choisit la plaine. O multitudes, quand
Prierez-vous que vos poumons éclatent ?

Pareil à ce troupeau, je flatte
L'irrespirable. Et pourtant me débats
Dès que mon sang m'étouffe en ce combat.

3

Revenez dans sept ans car
J'aurai fait peau neuve. L'art
De vivre, pour moi, consiste
À changer d'écorce. Triste
Captivité de mes os !
Ma peau tombe, dis-je. Saut
Dans l'inconnu. Ceux qui m'aiment
Pensent découvrir le même
Visage, masque déteint.

Autant lire sur le tain
Des miroirs une âme absente.
Tous les sept ans j'innocente
Ma chair quand d'horreur d'excès
Débride soudain l'abcès
Intérieur. Ma mémoire,
Perdant le fil d'une histoire
Sans valeur, me fait défaut.

2

People at altitudes suffocating
Choose the plain. O multitudes, when
Will you pray for your lungs to burst?

Like the flock, I flatter
The unbreathable yet struggle
The moment my blood smothers me in the fight.

3

Return in seven years
I shall have metamorphosed. The art
Of living, for me, consists
Of changing skins. Sad
Captivity of my bones!
I am shedding my skin, I say. Leap
Into the unknown. Those who love me
Think they see the same
Face, faded mask.

Might as well see, in the silvering
Of mirrors, an absent soul.
Every seven years I prove the innocence
Of my flesh, when excess in horror
Suddenly lances the abscess
Inside. My memory,
Losing the thread of a pointless
Story, fails me.

Je change de corps, de peau.
Qui me posséda regarde
Sans comprendre. Et moi je garde
Sous un oeil qu'il croit connaître
L'éclat de ce nouvel être.

I change body, skin.
Whoever possessed me looks
But doesn't understand. And I keep
An eye he thinks he knows,
On the brightness of this new being.

LE GEL, *extraits*

1

Visible ton haleine, tes pupilles
Trop largement ouvertes. C'est le jour
Qui les dilate, c'est pour toi que brille
Ce blanc total.
                    J'entre dans le séjour
Sans larmes. Tout liquide y prend des pierres
Le poids, l'éternité. Pleurs solennels !
Douceur niée avec l'eau ! Tes paupières
Connaîtront, lourdes, le pouvoir du sel.

4

Je m'allège, me décante.
Cerveau de vapeur nourri,
Vers le pôle qu'on t'aimante.

Le gel, précieux bistouri,
Met en lumière des plaies
Lentes à trouver, plus lentes
Encore à guérir. Il plante
D'un seul coup l'acier.
                    Supplée
Au manque de mots ! Nul cri
Pour cette douleur confondre.
Dans le corps, l'esprit s'effondre.
Corps, debout ! (Mais au mépris
Du vivant.) Sauve la face.
Corps, debout ! Le gel efface
Tout mystère. Quel éclat.

FROST

1

Visible your breath, your pupils
Too wide open. It is the day
That dilates them, and for you that this
Absolute white sparkles.
                    I enter the room
Dry-eyed. There, liquids take from the stones
Weight, eternity. Formal tears!
Gentleness disallowed by the water! Your eyelids
Will know, heavy, the power of salt.

4

I relax, become clearer.
Mind of nurtured vapour,
To the pole to which you are pulled.

The frost, precious scalpel,
Highlights wounds
Slow to find, slower
Still to heal. With one thrust
It implants the steel.
                    Offset
The lack of words! No cry
For this pain to join.
In the body, the spirit to distraught.
Body, stand straight! (Heedless
Of life though.) Save face.
Body, stand straight! The frost dispels
All mystery. What brilliance.

Héliotropes, lilas,
Fabuleuses fleurs d'un âge
Révolu. Le paysage
Qui m'attire n'a pour soi
Que la pureté du froid.

6

Inaltérable, unique, après la sombre
Splendeur du feu, après le dévorant
Désir, l'acier, le fer polaire, prend
Visage et s'illumine. D'ombre en ombre
J'errais, fuyant le brasier. Voici que
Mon corps se fige. Halte rude, gel !
(Dès autrefois un monument de sel
Ceignit le front des ruines.) Toi, musique
Propre au silence, rythme intérieur,
Que je perçoive dans la note unique,
Dans l'inhumaine matité, un chant
Presque fatal. Et que, sous le tranchant
Des lames, sous la glace, à roche fendre,
Je puisse enfin mon âme faire entendre.

8

Marqués du signe cristallin, porteurs de froid,
De flambeaux insolites,
Sans feu, sans dieu, voici les prêtres de la foi
Polaire, maigre élite
De survivants du pénultième hiver.
L'oeil d'insecte épargné par miracle, univers
Attentif au premier des signes ineffables
Du jour, ils dressent leur autel à votre table

Heliotropes, lilacs,
Fabulous flowers of an age
Gone by. The landscape
That draws me has for itself
Only the purity of cold.

6

Unchanging, unique, after the dark
Splendour of fire, after consuming
Desire, the steel, polar iron, takes on a
Face, lights up. From shadow to shadow
I roamed, fleeing the inferno. Then
My body freezes. Rude stop, frost!
(Of old a monument of salt
Girded the facade of the ruins.) You, music
Befitting silence, inner rhythm,
Let me see in the single note,
In the inhuman deadness, a near-fatal
Song. And let me, beneath the sharp edge
Of, beneath the ice, rock-breaking blades,
Be able at last to make my soul heard.

8

Marked by the crystalline sign, bearers of cold,
Of unusual torches,
Fireless, godless, come the priests of the polar
Faith, meagre elite
Of the survivors of the penultimate winter.
The insect eye by a miracle spared, universe
Alert to the first of the ineffable signs
Of day, they raise their altar at your table

Et, sur ce roc improvisé, pratiquent
Le rituel du sacerdoce antique.

9

Pour qui le bouc émissaire ?
L'holocauste ? Libations
Innommables : les viscères
Prescrits, le nécessaire
Appareil d'incantations !
Souille l'offrande, lacère
La victime. Sois sincère
Jusqu'à la profanation.

10

A quelle puissance occulte
Vont ces gestes ? J'ai la foi
Souveraine. Il n'est de culte
Qui puisse arrêter mon choix.
Olibans mâles, adultes
Genévriers, sous mes doigts
L'encens devient une insulte.
Le trône que j'aperçois
Au sommet de vivre exulte
Sous le givre. Je ne crois
Qu'à l'éternité du froid.

11

Diamant de l'âme, feu
Solitaire, taille lente
Du carbone qui se veut
Soleil, l'étoile filante

And, on this improvised rock, carry out
The ritual of the ancient priesthood.

9

For whom the scapegoat?
The holocaust? Unspeakable
Libations: the prescribed
Viscera, the necessary
Incantatory apparatus!
Defile the offering, lacerate
The victim. Be sincere
To the point of profanation.

10

To which occult power
Do these gestures go? My faith
Is supreme. No religion
Can stay my choice.
Male olibana, adult
Junipers, in my fingers
Incense turns to insult.
The throne I see
At the height of living, rejoices
Beneath the ice. I believe
Only in the eternity of cold.

11

Diamond of the soul, solitary
Fire, slow tunnel
Of carbon that thinks it is
Sun, the shooting star

Jalouse ton bloc. Joyau
Péremptoire, mille faces
Te sculptent. Mais le noyau
Banal ? Au fleuve de glace
Il prend forme et dureté.
Rose double, seul t'use
Ta poussière. Pureté
Secrète, en la boue incluse,
Rien ne peut dissoudre ton
Evidence. De ta griffe
Marque tous les corps, limons
Ou marbres. Leurs hiéroglyphcs
Témoigneront de toi. Mais
Nul ne trouvera son signe
Inscrit dans ton eau. Jamais
Terrestre objet ne fut digne
De te frôler. Or, je sens
Ta présence, me traverse
Ton éclat. Ou, je pressens
L'alluvial trésor, l'inverse
Paysage qu'un cristal
Multiplie. Ah ! je devine
L'indomptable, l'oeil frontal
Ouvert aux clartés divines.

Envies your block. Peremptory
Gem, a thousand faces
Sculpt you. And the banal
Stone? At the river of ice
It takes shape, becomes hard.
Double rose, alone you use up
Your dust. Secret
Purity, in the enclosed mud,
Nothing can dissolve your
Evidence. With your claw
Score all bodies, silt
And marble. Their hieroglyphs
Are testimony to you. But
None will find his sign
Inscribed in your water. Never
Was earthly object worthy
Of touching you. Yet, I sense
Your presence, your radiance
Penetrates me. Yes, I foresee
The alluvial treasure, the reversed
Landscape that a crystal
Multiplies. Ah! I envision
The indomitable, the frontal eye
Opens to all divine lights.

Rien n'existe

Rien n'existe. Pain, mensonge
Nourricier du songe corps.
Et le ver frileux qui ronge
Tes saisons — mensonge encor.

Rien n'est concret. Oeil, image,
Miroir du mirage mer.
De l'horizon ligne sage,
Trahison. Trompeurs amers.

Sous le ciel et sur la terre
Tant de choses. Rien de sûr.
Rien de pur, sauf le mystère.
Rien de vrai, sinon l'obscur.

Niez vos mains, votre bouche,
L'eau, le vent, le jour, la nuit.
Tout ce que je vois, je touche,
Tout ce que je tiens me fuis.

NOTHING EXISTS

Nothing exists. Bread, a lie
That nourishes the body-dream.
And the timorous worm that gnaws
At your seasons — another lie.

Nothing is concrete. Eye, image,
Mirror of the ocean-mirage.
From the horizon's wise line,
Treachery. Bitter deceivers.

Beneath the sky, on the earth
So many things. Nothing sure.
Nothing pure, save the mystery.
Nothing true, but the obscure.

Deny your hands, your mouth,
The water, wind, day and night.
All that I see, I touch,
All that I hold, escapes me.

L'ALOÈS, *extract*

Une fois tous les cent ans
L'aloès fleurit. Mon temps
Connaît la même fortune.
Tant de jours perdus pour une
Minute vivante, tant
De saisons pour un instant
Parfait, arraché de force.
O mon temps, sous quelle écorce
Caches-tu l'éternité
Pendant que, pour me quitter,
Pour reprendre ton empire,
Chaque fois que je respire
Tu t'échappes un peu plus ?

Souffle qui ma vie élus
Voici trente ans, pour que prenne
Conscience un corps, refrène
Ton allure. Je n'ai pas
Vécu. Sans cesse mes pas
M'ont porté, ma bouche pleine
De vent perdait son haleine.
J'occupais ma place, j'ai
Travaillé, dormi, mangé.
Je cherchais à me connaître.
Je n'ai rencontré qu'un être
Stupide et bruyant. Sa voix
Disait *je* parlant de moi.

THE ALOE

Once every hundred years
The aloe flowers. My time
Shares the same fate.
So many days squandered for one
Blithe moment, so many
Seasons for one perfect
Instant, taken by force.
Oh my time, under which skin
Have you concealed eternity
While, to leave me,
To regain your empire,
With each breath I take,
You flee a little further?

Breath elected by my life
Thirty years ago, so that a body
Could become conscious, slow
Your pace. I have not
Lived. Ceaselessly my feet
Have carried me, my mouth full
Of wind grew breathless.
I filled my space, I have
Worked, slept, eaten.
I sought to know myself.
All I met was a being,
Stupid and noisy, whose voice
Said *I* when speaking of me.

QUATRE MILLE JOURS

Quatre mille jours,
Quatre mille jours, quatre mille nuits,
Nous avons partagé le lit, la table,
Bu aux mêmes fontaines, tiré l'eau des mêmes puits
— Et l'eau n'était pas toujours claire mais
Transparentes étaient nos mains.

Nos mains, nos yeux et notre coeur commun.
Où est-il à présent ? Il a cessé de battre.
Quatre mille levers de lune, quatre
Mille nuits sans savoir ce que veut dire « seul ».

A présent je le sais, je me trouve à l'extrême
Pointe de mon chagrin, où l'on n'est plus que soi,
Désespérément soi enfermé en soi-même.

FOUR THOUSAND DAYS

Four thousand days,
Four thousand days, four thousand nights,
We shared a bed, a table,
Drank from the same fountains, drew water from the same wells
— And though the water was not always clear
Transparent were our hands.

Our hands, our eyes, our mutual heart.
Where is it now? It has ceased to beat.
Four thousand moonrises, four
Thousand nights not knowing the meaning of 'alone'.

Now I know. I am at the very
Edge of grief, where one is but oneself,
Desperately oneself trapped in oneself.

LORSQUE TU TE REGARDES DANS LA GLACE

Lorsque tu te regardes dans la glace
En te disant : « C'est moi », il vient toujours
Un moment de panique. Es-tu en face,
Es-tu ici ? Quid de ce moi venu un jour,
Dont il ne restera plus rien. Oui, des douzaines
De photos, une voix. Cire et papier. Moi, là-dedans ?
Que saura-t-on de mes amours et de mes peines ?
Plus de faims, plus de peurs, pas même un mal de dents.
Silencieux le sang, morte à jamais l'haleine,
Douce haleine brouillant aujourd'hui le miroir
Où mon être apparent a cessé de se voir.

WHEN YOU GAZE AT YOURSELF IN THE MIRROR

When you gaze at yourself in the mirror
And say: 'That's me', there is always
A moment of panic. Is that you,
Or is this you? Quid of that me which arrived one day,
Nothing of which will survive. Yes, dozens
Of photos, a voice. Wax and paper. Me, in there?
What will be left of my passions and pains?
No yearnings, no fears, not even a toothache.
Silent the blood, forever dead the breath,
Sweet breath now misting the mirror
Where my visible being has ceased to see itself.

TU N'ES PAS NÉ...

Tu n'es pas né. Se sont ouverts les yeux du corps,
Non ceux de l'être qui l'habite, dont j'ignore
L'âge, le lieu le nom secret, cet être encore
Inexprimé, inexprimable, que dévore
Le temps.
                Tu n'es pas né, mais quelque chose luit
Au fond de toi, rond de clarté sur le mur lisse
De ton visage intérieur, point dans la nuit
Sévère de ton moi dernier. (Parfois s'y glisse
Un rayon, d'où venu ?)
                        Tu n'es pas né, tu vis
En deçà du possible jour qui ne t'éclaire
Que parcimonieusement, tu ne gravis
Que les premières marches de ton seuil, tu erres
Autour de ta maison sans pouvoir la cerner.
Tu n'es pas né. Cette chaleur, pourtant, qui couve,
Brûlant ta chair et tes saisons ?
                        Tu n'es pas né.
Les yeux du corps sont grands ouverts mais ils ne trouvent
Qu'un ciel avare, qu'un soleil intermittent
Au noir promis. D'ores promis à la totale
Obscurité. Les yeux du corps.

YOU ARE NOT BORN

You are not born. Open were the eyes of the body,
Not those of the being who dwells there, of whom I know
Not the age, the place, the secret name, a being still
Unexpressed, inexpressible, that is devoured by
Time.
You are not born, though something glows
Deep within you, patch of light on the smooth wall
Of your inner face, speck in the harsh
Night of your last me. (Occasionally a ray
Creeps in , from where?)
                                        You are not born, you live
This side of the possible day that lights you albeit
Grudgingly, you climb just
The first few steps to your door, you stroll
Around your house never able to encircle it.
You are not born. The heat, however, that smoulders,
Burning your flesh and your seasons?
You are not born.
The eyes of the body are wide open but all they find
Is a covetous sky, a sun alternating
With the promised dark. Already promised to the total
Darkness. The eyes of the body.

GRAIN DE SABLE...

Grain de sable sur la plage,
Dans l'océan goutte d'eau,
Rien n'est à toi. Sauf l'usage
Provisoire de ta peau.

GRAIN OF SAND

Grain of sand on the beach,
In the ocean drop of water,
Nothing is yours. Save the provisional
Use of your skin.

LA QUARANTAINE...

La quarantaine.   Absurde promontoire.
Et les dieux lares renversés, et le passé grain de millet.
Grain de millet, grain de sésame.   Notre histoire
Si longue à vivre ne remplit pas un feuillet.

Si longue à vivre et si vite écoulée.
Dans la caverne de voleurs des jours enfuis :
Quarante jarres vides.   Aujourd'hui
J'ai lu le conte et la pierre est roulée.

FORTY

Forty.   Absurd promontory.
And the toppled household gods, and the millet seed past.
Millet seed, sesame seed.   Our history
So long in the making does not fill a page.

So long in the making yet so soon elapsed.
In the cave of the thieves of days gone by:
Forty empty vessels.   Today
I have read the tale and the stone has been rolled.

LIEU COMMUN, *extracts*

5

Un taximan meurt à New York pour une fille de Dublin.
Un poète écrit vingt-cinq chants pour quelqu'un qui ne sait pas lire.
Il n'a pas plus de chance avec son coeur qu'avec sa lyre :
L'un comme l'autre ne valent plus un shilling.

Au cours du jour, c'est une guitare électrique
Qui fait fureur, aux mains d'un Eros bon marché.
Les flèches de l'amour à prix unique
Ne tentent plus le juvénile archer.

Pour une fille de New York un poète meurt à Dublin.
Un taximan analphabète chante une épopée.
A qui conterez-vous vos peines, orphelins
Du rêve ? On a vendu Sirius et Cassiopée.

13

Si la rose,
            Si la rose
S'ouvre avec le réséda
Dans les jardins où reposent
Ceux que l'ange noir borda.

Si la rose,
            Si la rose
Ensemble, tous allons voir
Ce que, les paupières close,
On peut lire dans le noir.

COMMONPLACE

5

A cab driver dies in New York for a girl from Dublin.
A poet writes twenty-five songs for someone who can't read.
He is no luckier with his heart than his lyre:
Neither one nor the other is worth a shilling.

During the day, it's the electric guitar
That's all the rage, in the hands of a low-cost Eros.
The arrows of love from the pound shop
No longer appeal to the young archer.

For a girl from New York a poet dies in Dublin.
An illiterate cab driver sings a ballad.
Who will you tell of your grief, orphans
Of the dream? Sirius and Cassiopeia are sold.

13

If the rose,
            If the rose
Opens with the mignonette
In the gardens where repose
Those the dark angel tucked in.

If the rose,
            If the rose
Together, all, let us go and see
What, eyelids closed,
We can read in the dark.

TESTAMENT

Pour Alain Bosquet

A l'enfant que je n'ai pas eu
Mais que d'un homme je reçus
Septante fois sept fois et davantage, à l'enfant sage
Dont je formai le souffle et le visage
Sept fois septante fois dans un ventre pareil
Au mien, par des nuits rouges de soleil,
Par des jours cristallins d'aurore boréale,
A l'enfant dont je porte en moi les initiales
Secrètes, ainsi que ton nom, Yahvé,
Enfant conçu, toujours inachevé,
Qu'on me fait, que je fais, à chaque fois que j'aime,
Qui se réfait en moi pour donner un poème,
A l'enfant qui ne viendra pas
Clore mes yeux, choisir l'ultime drap,
Marcher derrière mon poids d'os, de cendres,
Me regarder dans la fosse descendre,
A cet enfant je lègue devant Dieu, devant
Les hommes et mon chien, devant le jour vivant
(Qui n'est que parce que je suis et qui mourra
Comme je meurs) je lègue, pour autant que se pourra,
Pour autant qu'il en fasse usage en lieu et place
De moi, ses père et mère en un seul être pris,
Je lègue tous mes biens de chair, d'esprit,
De temps toujours compté et d'illusoire espace :

Le coin de ciel que j'ai scruté en vain,
L'arpent de terre où j'usai mes semelles,
Les quatre murs entre quoi je me tins,
Les six cloisons qui leur seront jumelles,

TESTAMENT

For Alain Bosquet

To the child I never had
But who from a man I received
Seventy times seven times and more, to the well-behaved child
Whose breath and face I shaped
Seven times seventy times in a womb
Similar to mine, during nights made red by the sun,
During days made crystalline by the aurora borealis,
To the child whose secret initials I carry
Inside me, together with your name, Yahweh,
Child conceived, forever unfinished,
That is made, that I make, each time I love,
That comes unmade in me to yield a poem,
To the child who will not be there
To close my eyes, to choose my last sheet,
To walk behind my burden of bones, of ashes,
To see me lowered into the grave,
To this child I bequeath before God, before
Man and my dog, before the living day
(Which is because I am and which will die
When I die) I bequeath, as long as it's possible,
As long as it's used for and on behalf
Of me, his father and mother captured in one single being,
I bequeath all my goods of flesh, of spirit,
Of constantly counted time and illusory space:

The patch of sky I examined in vain,
The plot of land where I wore out my soles,
The four walls within which I resided,
The six partitions that acted as twins,

L'argent qui m'est entre les doigts filé
— Pour le plaisir que j'eus à le répandre —
Le faux savoir qu'on me crut refiler
— Pour le bonheur d'aussitôt désapprendre —

Les jours passés que je n'ai pas vécus,
Les jours vécus près desquels suis passée,
Le temps mortel à quoi j'ai survécu
L'heure éternelle et pourtant effacée,

L'amour jeté dont j'ignorais le prix,
L'amour donné à qui ne sut le rendre,
L'amour offert qu'aussitôt je repris,
L'amour perdu qu'on voit dehors attendre.

A l'enfant que je n'ai pas eu,
Que pourtant j'ai, de ma semence
Formé, dedans ma chair conçu,
Dont chaque étreinte parfait l'existence,
A cet enfant je lègue pour le mieux mais surtout pour
Le pire, ce que m'a prêté le jour :

Le moi dont à crédit je fais usage
A des taux qui dépassent mes moyens,
Dont je n'ai pu choisir ni le visage,
Ni le sexe (il faut prendre ce qui vient) :

Un cerveau creux dans une tête pleine,
Un corps trop mou sur des os trop puissants,
Un sang trop vif pour une courte haleine,
Un coeur trop doux pour ce furieux sang,

The money that vanished in my fingers
— For the joy I got from spreading it round —
The false lore they thought they were leaving me
— For the bliss of instantly unlearning —

The days that are past that I have not lived,
The days that lived so close to where I passed,
The fatal period but which I survived,
The time never-ending yet blotted out,

Love cast off whose value I never knew,
Love shown to those unable to respond,
Love offered that I instantly withdrew,
Love lost that can be seen waiting outside.

To the child I never had,
And yet which from my seed I
Formed, within my flesh conceived,
Whose every embrace perfects existence,
To this child I bequeath for better but especially for
Worse, what the day has granted me:

The me I use on credit
At rates I cannot afford,
And for whom I was able to choose neither the face
Nor the sex (you have to take what you're given):

An empty brain in a full head,
A body too soft on bones too strong,
A blood too hot for a breath that is short,
A heart too faint for my furious blood,

Des pieds qui n'ont soulevé que poussière
Des bras surpris d'avoir étreint le vent,
Des genoux pris au piège des prières,
Des mains restant vides comme devant,

Des yeux fermés sur un côté des choses,
— Cette moitié qui fait à tous défaut —
Des yeux ouverts sous leurs paupières closes
Et, dans le noir, voyant plus qu'il n'en faut.

A l'enfant que je n'ai pas eu
Je lègue enfin, pour qu'il en tienne
Bien compte, pour qu'il s'en souvienne
Par contumance, lorsque sera décousu
L'ourlet de mon passage sur l'étoffe ancienne :

Les quinze choses que jamais je n'ai pu faire :

Courber le front devant plus grand que moi,
Marcher sur plus petit, montrer du doigt,
Crier avec la foule, ou bien me taire,
Reconnaître parmi les Blancs le Noir,
Choisir dix justes, nommer un coupable,
Trouver telle attitude convenable,
Lire un autre que moi dans les miroirs,
Conjuguer l'amour à plusieurs personnes,
Résister à la tentation, blesser exprès,
Rester dans l'indécis, dire Cambronne
Au lieu de merde, qui est plus français.

Feet that have raised nothing but dust
Arms surprised at having held the wind,
Knees caught in the trap of prayers,
Hands as empty as they were before,

Eyes shut to one side of things,
— The half that is despite all —
Eyes open behind their closed lids
Seeing, in the dark, more than they need.

To the child I never had
I finally bequeath, so that he may really take it
Into account, so that he may remember it
In absentia, when the hem of my passage
On the ancient fabric is unstitched:

The fifteen things I was never able to do:

Bow my head to one greater than me,
Trample the lesser, point my finger,
Shout with the mob, or hold my tongue,
Distinguish a Black man from the Whites,
Pick ten just men, name a culprit,
Find such an attitude acceptable,
See another not me in mirrors,
Combine the love of several people,
Resist temptation, deliberately injure,
Remain indecisive, say Cambronne
Instead of merde, which is more French.

JOURNAL DU SCRIBE, *extract*

Tantième expédition dans le Delta,
Où le tronc du fleuve se fend, où se séparent
Ses bras.
comme l'arbre du sang, celui du flux
de tous côtés dirige ses vaisseaux.

Sur le bateau de Pharaon nul ne s'égare.
Mais moi, dans mon canot de papyrus ?

Quel courant vais-je suivre, vers
quelles îles de sable, quels roseaux ?

Tous les chemins conduisent à la mer.

*

Dans le Livre des Morts où je devrais
écrire tes hauts faits, Thoutmès,
d'autres noms apparaissent, d'autres traits
jaillissent, tout à coup, de mon calame.

Je ne sais pas quels signes j'ai tracés.
Je ne reconnais pas ces hiéroglyphes.

Mais l'esclave illettré qui m'éventait
se penche et lit, par-dessus mon épaule,
dans une langue dont j'ignore tout.

*

J'écris le grain et vous lisez la faux.
J'écris la faux et vous lisez le pain.
J'écris le pain et vous lisez le sang.

THE DIARY OF A SCRIBE

One of many expeditions in the Delta,
Where the trunk of the river splits, where its arms
divide.
Like the tree of blood, that of the flux
steers its vessels from all sides.

On the Pharaoh's ship no one strays.
But I, in my papyrus canoe?

Which current shall I follow, to
which islands of sand, which bulrushes?

All roads lead to the sea.

*

In the Book of the Dead in which I should
record your great deeds, Thutmosis,
other names appear, other features
emerge, suddenly, from my calamus.

I do not know what signs I have drawn.
I do not recognise these hieroglyphs.

But the illiterate slave who was fanning me
stoops and over my shoulder, reads
in a tongue unknown to me.

*

I write seed and you read scythe.
I write scythe and you read bread.
I write bread and you read blood.

J'écris le sang et vous lisez la vie.
J'écris la vie et vous lisez le grain.

*

Miroir qui se répète à l'infini :
le soleil brille dans nos yeux comme dans ceux
des bêtes,
comme dans chaque goutte de rosée.
La lune s'y reflète aussi,
et des étoiles depuis longtemps mortes,
et l'univers toujours en train de se créer.

Chacun contient en soi le Tout
qui est peut-être aussi le Rien.

*

Les silencieux animaux domestiques,
et leur patience, et leur confiance dans la main
du maître. Et leur cruel
destin.

L'agneau broutant près de sa mère
quand le caresse un rayon de soleil
voit-il déjà le reflet du couteau ?

*

Couteau du sacrifice, couteau des
circoncisions.

Couteau qui coupe le cordon
ombolical.

I write blood and you read life.
I write life and you read seed.

*

Mirror duplicated into infinity:
the sun shines in our eyes as it does in those of
the animals,
as it does in each drop of dew.
The moon too is reflected there,
and the stars a long time dead,
and the universe forever recreating itself.

Each of us contains within ourselves the All
that is perhaps also the Nothing.

*

The silent domestic animals
and their patience, and their confidence in the hand
of the master. And their cruel
destiny.

The lamb grazing near its mother,
as a sunbeam caresses it
does it already see the flash of the knife?

*

Knife sacrificial, knife
circumcisional.

Knife that cuts the umbilical
cord.

Acier marquant le mâle à sa naissance
après l'avoir détaché de la femme.

Couteau, séparation.
Plaie ouverte, suture
et noeud.

Bistouri purificateur.
Fil de l'épée.
Acier.

Tranche dans le vif même si
j'implore grâce.

*

Pour vivre, il faut planter un arbre, il faut
faire un enfant, bâtir une maison.

J'ai seulement regardé l'eau
qui passe en nous disant que tout s'écoule.

J'ai seulement cherché le feu
qui brûle en nous disant que tout s'éteint.

J'ai seulement suivi le vent
qui fuit en nous disant que tout se perd.

Je n'ai rien semé dans la terre
qui reste en nous disant : je vous attends.

*

Regarde la vérité

Steel branding the male at birth
having severed him from the woman.

Knife, separation.
Open wound, suture
and knot.

Purifying scalpel.
Edge of the sword.
Steel.

Cut into the living flesh though
I beg for mercy.

*

To live, you need to plant a tree, you need
to beget a child, to build a house.

All I did was watch the water
that flows telling us that all will trickle away.

All I did was seek the fire
that burns telling us that all will be extinguished.

All I did was follow the wind
that flees telling us that all will die down.

I have sown nothing in the earth
that remains telling us: I'll wait for you.

*

Look truth

bien en face pour lui faire
lentement baisser les yeux.

*

Mon ami Qohélet l'a dit
dans un livre appelé l'Ecclésiaste :
tout ce qui vit sur terre est vanité.

Nous, scribes, nous gonflons comme des outres
dès que monte le lait de la louange,
dès qu'on nous offre un maigre encens,
dès qu'on élève une colonne à notre nom.

Bien que parfois j'éprouve quelque
démangeaison de ce côté, Seigneur,
que je ne sois sensible qu'au prurit
de ton absence, que ma peau
ne se colore qu'à l'approche de ton ombre, que mes os
ne se rassemblent qu'au creux de ta main.

*

Mon pain, je ne l'ai pas produit.
L'eau que je bois, d'autres l'ont apportée.
Je ne sais rien du four, du puits,
du sol fendu par le soleil. J'écris
à l'ombre, au rythme lent des chasse-mouches
et ma fatigue est sans odeur.

Les paysans, eux, sentent fort,
et les esclaves nourris d'ail,
et les marins poissés de sel,
et les marchands frottés de vent,

straight in the eye to make it
slowly look down.

*

My friend Qohelet said it
in a book called Ecclesiastes:
all life on earth is futile.

We scribes, we swell like goatskins
the moment the milk of praise is poured,
the moment some measly incense is offered us,
the moment a column is erected in our name.

Although there are times I experience some
longing in that area, Lord,
though I am only sensitive to the pruritis
of your absence, though my skin
only colours at the approach of your shadow, though my bones
only come together in the hollow of your hand.

*

My bread, I did not make it.
The water I drink, others brought.
I know nothing of the oven, of the well,
of the earth cracked by the sun. I write
in the shade, to the slow rhythm of fly-whisks
and my weariness is without odour.

Peasants, they have a powerful smell,
and garlic-fed slaves,
and salt-sticky sailors,
and wind-chafed merchants,

et les soldats suants de peur.

Le poids du jour a leur odeur.

Mais relisant le signe qui
les nomme, au long de mes rouleaux,
bien que je l'aie tracé avec
une main pure, parfumée,
je ne sens plus que cette odeur.

*

Le fou habite le présent
et le sage l'éternité.

Je dis que le présent n'existe pas,
qu'entre hier et demain nous avançons
sur un fil plus léger
que ceux tissés par l'araignée,
qu'entre demain et hier
il n'y a que l'espace d'une haleine.

Non, le présent n'existe pas.
C'est seulement un mur qui nous traverse
jusqu'à l'instant où c'est nous qui le traversons.

*

Tantième expédition parmi les hommes.
Dans chacun d'eux il y en a
sept fois sept mille, dans chacun
le père de son père jusqu'à la
génération première.

and soldiers sweating with fear.

The weight of the day carries their odour.

But rereading the symbol that
names them all through my scrolls,
and although I have traced it with
a pure and perfumed hand,
all I can smell is this odour.

*

The madman lives in the present,
the wiseman in eternity.

I say that the present does not exist,
that between yesterday and tomorrow we move
along a thread lighter
than the one the spider spins,
that between tomorrow and yesterday
there is only the space of a breath.

No, the present does not exist.
It is no more than a wall that passes through us
until the moment it is we who pass through it

*

One of many expeditions amongst men.
In each of them there are
seven times seven thousand, in each
the father of his father right back to the
first generation.

J'étais déjà dans ta semence, Adam.
Je me souviens du ventre d'Ève.

Sept fois sept mille dans chacun.

Mais à travers tout je suis moi.
Par mon seul souffle je respire
et dans mon sang multiple je
demeure unique.

*

Je suis ton scribe, Pharaon,
mais aussi le bénédictin du Mont Cassin
traçant le nom des morts sur la rotule,
l'homme en robe safran de Bodh Gayâ
calligraphiant les huit nobles chemins,
le sorcier noir interprétant les signes.

Je suis le chroniqueur des Hohenstaufen
et celui des Plantagenet, le narrateur,
de la plus vieille saga scandinave.

Je suis le secrétaire du parti des hommes.
Je tiens registre d'arrivée et de départ,
livre de comptes du tonneau des Danaïdes
et du travail de Sisuphos. Je suis
le cryptographe des fléaux de Dieu,
l'historien des cent génocides,
l'archiviste de la douleur,
le grand mémorialiste du silence

Je suis Jésus écrivant sur le sable.

I was already in your seed, Adam.
I remember Eve's womb.

Seven times seven thousand in each.

But through all of this I am me.
With my own breath I breathe
and in my composite blood I
remain unique.

*

I am your scribe Pharaoh,
but also the Benedictine from Monte Cassino
recording the names of the dead on the patella,
the man from Bodh Gayâ in the saffron robe
calligraphing the Eightfold Path,
the black sorcerer deciphering signs.

I am the chronicler of the Hohenstaufen
and Plantagenets, the narrator
of the first Scandinavian saga.

I am the secretary of the party of men.
I keep the register of arrivals and departures,
the accounts book of the Sisyphean task
and the work of Sisyphus. I am
the cryptographer of the scourge of God,
the historian of the hundred genocides,
the archivist of pain,
the great biographer of silence

I am Jesus writing in the sand.

*

Mon maître est le peseur de mots.
Il me dit : rien ne vaut la page blanche.
L'encre salit le papyrus.

Maître, c'est vrai.
Je sais que mes rouleaux seront poussière,
que mes écrits s'effaceront.

Pourtant mon rôle est de nommer les choses,
qu'elles durent un jour ou bien mille ans.

Je nomme, donc je suis.

Les nommant, je me dis que rien n'existe
mais je crois exister.

*

Mon maître est le vanneur de vent.
Il garde les mains vides, il secoue
la poussière de ses souliers.
Jamais il ne s'arrête, en aucun lieu
ne s'établit.

Heureux les pauvres en esprit, dit-il. Et : tiens-toi prêt

Seigneur, je l'ai toujours été.
Moi qui reste attaché
à tout, comme la chèvre à son piquet,
le pauvre à son lopin de terre,
tu sais que pourtant je suis prêt.

*

My master is the weigher of words.
He tells me: nothing exceeds the blank page.
Ink sullies the papyrus.

Master it is true.
I know that my scrolls will be dust,
that my writings will fade.

And yet it is my role to name things,
whether they last a day or a thousand years.

I name, therefore I am.

Naming them, I tell myself nothing exists
but I believe I exist.

*

My master is the winnower of wind.
He keeps his hands empty, shakes
the dust from his shoes.
Never does he stop, nowhere
does he settle.

Blessed are the poor of spirit, he says. And: be ready

Lord, I always have been.
I who remain attached
to everything, like the goat to its stake,
the poor man to his plot of land,
you know that I am nevertheless ready.

Je te suivrai quand s'ouvrira la porte.

*

Je viens d'avant le souffle du commencement.
Je n'aurai pas de fin.
Je, c'est-à-dire le
principe qui m'anime
et qui poursuivra son
voyage en me quittant.

*

Tantième expédition au fond de moi.
Sentinelle, voici le jour.

I shall follow you when the door opens.

*

I come from before the breath of the beginning.
I shall have no end.
I, that is to say
the principle that drives me
and that will continue on its
journey when it leaves me.

*

One of many expeditions to the depths of myself.
Sentry, the morning comes.

LE BILLET DE PASCAL, *extracts*

Joie, joie, joie, pleurs de joie

En l'an de grâce mil six cent cinquante-quatre,
un lundi, le jour vingt-troisième de novembre,
fête de saint Clément, Blaise Pascal
connut son illumination.

Il méditait quand il fut à lui-même
ôté.
De dix heures et demie du soir
jusqu'à minuit et demi environ,
Blaise n'est plus Pascal mais tout entier
exultation,
renonciation totale et douce,
embarqué hors de tout pari,
pris sans frayeur dans les espaces infinis.

Sur un billet qu'il conserva toute sa vie
dans la doublure de son vêtement,
qu'est-ce qu'il écrivit ensuite ? Feu
et *Dereliquerunt me fontem aquae vivae.*

Joie, pleurs de joie.

Entre Bruxelles et Charleroi, treize heures quinze,
le pied léger sur l'accélérateur,
les yeux actifs, l'esprit ailleurs,
sur fond de prés et d'autoroute,
de lessives, de laids clochers,
d'agressives publicités,
entre la fragile anecdote
du jour, l'incertain bulletin du temps,

76

PASCAL'S NOTE

Joy, joy, joy, tears of joy.

In the year of our Lord sixteen fifty four,
a Monday, the twenty-third day of November.
the feast of St. Clement, Blaise Pascal
experienced spiritual enlightenment.

He was meditating when he was taken from
himself.
From half past ten at night
to around half past midnight,
Blaise was no longer Pascal but absolute
bliss,
sweet and utter renunciation,
transported far from all bets,
conveyed undismayed to infinite space.

In the note he kept all his life
in the lining of his clothes.
what did he then write? Fire :
and *Dereliquerunt me fontem aquae vivae.*

Joy, tears of joy.

Between Brussels and Charleroi, thirteen fifteen,
my foot light on the accelerator,
eyes vigilant, mind elsewhere,
against a backdrop of fields and motorway,
washing, ugly bell towers,
obtrusive advertising,
in amongst the fragile thought
for the day, the unreliable weather forecast,

l'horreur des génocides, le huitième
mariage d'une star sur le déclin,
les nouvelles sans lien, (sans lien ?
Vingt-cinq mille enfants chaque jour meurent de faim,
on a déjà vendu cent millions de poupées Barbie),
joie, pleurs de joie,
un ange est là.

Son souffle sur ma nuque, son regard
droit dans le mien, comme un couteau.
Il me dénude jusqu'à l'os,
fouille la braise de mon sang,
me livre aux flammes.

Dans la doublure de son vêtement,
Monsieur Pascal garde la cendre
de ce tison qui l'a brûlé.

Quel objet emporteriez-vous
sur un îlot du Pacifique,
dans un hospice de vieillards,
au fond du bloc stérile d'un mouroir,
entre les murs d'une prison,
les barbelés d'un camp ?

L'étui de buis en forme de patène que je traîne
avec moi, depuis quarante ans,
de notre vieille Europe aux Amériques,
et du mur des Lamentations
à la source africaine où les lions
vont s'abreuver environ les six heures.

Sous le verre cassé, deux minuscules
éclats, l'un de la seule

the horrors of genocide, the eighth
marriage of a star in decline,
unrelated news items (unrelated?
Every day, twenty-five thousand children die of hunger,
to date a hundred million Barbie dolls have sold),
joy, tears of joy,
there is an angel.

Its breath on my neck, its eyes
piercing mine like a knife.
It strips me down to the bone,
rummages in the embers of my blood,
delivers me to the flames.

In the lining of his clothes,
Mister Pascal keeps the ash
of the brand that burned him.

What object would you take
to a desert island,
to an old people's home,
to deep within the sterile block of a hospice,
inside the walls of a prison,
the barbed wire of a camp?

The paten-shaped boxwood case I have carted around
with me for forty years,
from our old Europe to the Americas,
and from the Wailing Wall
to the African spring where the lion
goes to drink around six.

Under the cracked glass, two tiny
splinters, one from the one

et véritable croix du Christ (ses corpuscules
connus suffiraient à peupler une forêt)
et l'autre, d'un morceau de Benoît Labre.

— Un souvenir, en quelque sorte ? — Une relique.
Seul bien reçu de ma grand-mère
qui, d'ailleurs, n'en avait pas d'autre.

Etui de buis patiné par le temps,
médaillon si souvent baisé par cette bouche
dont j'ai vu s'échapper le dernier souffle.

Elle respire à peine, elle réclame
un prêtre, se confesse.
Il s'en va, les yeux pleins de larmes,
à croire que c'était lui le pécheur.
Et, quand il est parti,
bras ouverts, elle se redresse sur son lit.

Qui donc voit-elle en ce moment ?
Sa dure mère, son père dément,
sa soeur étreinte par la camisole
de force ? (La charrette aux chevaux blancs,
celle qui vient chercher les fous, les folles,
combien de fois m'en a-t-elle parlé ?
Et des petits bordés dans leur cercueil ?
Les petits que peut-être elle aperçoit
passé le seuil ? Clémence, ma grand-mère, illuminée,
regard fixé sur la porte fermée).

Deux guerres, sept enfants,
des kilomètres de tricot, des tonnes de lessive.
O fontem aquae vivae !
Le coeur usé jusqu'au trognon, dit le docteur.

and only true cross of Christ (whose known
corpuscles are enough to populate a forest)
and the other from a piece of Benoît Labre.

— A kind of souvenir? — A relic.
Only possession to come from my grandmother
who, what is more, had no others.

Boxwood case shiny with age,
medal kissed so often by the mouth
whose last breath I saw drawn.

She's barely breathing, asks for
a priest, confesses.
He leaves, eyes so full of tears,
you'd think he was the sinner.
And when he's gone,
she sits up in bed arms spread wide.

So who does she see now?
Her cruel mother, her mad father,
her sister embraced by a strait
jacket? (The white-horse-drawn cart,
the one that comes to fetch the mad,
how often did she talk to me about it?
And about the little ones snug in their coffins?
The little ones she can maybe see
beyond the threshold? Clémence, my grandmother, enlightened,
stares at the closed door).

Two wars, seven children,
miles of knitting, tons of washing.
O fontem aquae vivae!
Heart worn to the core, said the doctor.

Et le vicaire à la soutane vert-de-gris : c'est une sainte.

Une sainte ? Je ne sais pas.
Toute sa vie elle a brûlé. Brûlures
des gifles maternelles, de la faim,
des mains couvertes d'engelures,
du mépris qui la fait rougir,
de l'homme accueilli sans plaisir,
de la morgue puérile des patrons,
du gel qui raidit les torchons,
de l'ignorance au dos courbé, de la
crainte des fautes attisée
par le curé qui tonne en chaire.

A genoux sur le carrelage plus souvent
que sur les chaises de l'église,
pour eau bénite le gras des vaisselles,
pour goupillon, une brosse à chiendent,
pour corporal, sa serpillière,
frottant le sale, effaçant la misère
et le péché — *asperges me* —
que je te lave avec l'hysope, te
fasse plus blanche que la neige.

Les bras ouverts, Clémence, elle s'en va.
A l'instant où se fige son haleine,
ô fontem, fontem,
je vois, sur son visage,
ce que j'ai su, plus tard, être l'extase,
ô fontem aquae vivae.

« Hors du monde sensible et de soi-même »
comme chez la Thérèse du Bernin,
dans le regard de quelques suppliciés

A saint, said the vicar, in his verdigris cassock.

A saint? I don't know.
A lifetime of burning. The burn
of a mother's slaps, of hunger,
of chilblain-covered hands,
of the contempt that left her flushed,
of the man received without pleasure,
of the childish conceit of her masters,
of the frost that stiffened her dishcloths,
of back-breaking ignorance, of the
fear of faults, fuelled
by the priest thundering from the pulpit.

Kneeling on tiles more often
than the pew of a church,
washing up grease, her holy water,
a scrubbing brush, her aspergillum,
a floorcloth, her corporal-cloth,
rubbing the dirt, obliterating wretchedness
and sin — *asperges me* —
let me wash you with hyssop, make
you whiter that snow.

Arms spread wide, Clémence, she leaves.
The instant her breath stops,
o fontem, fontem,
I see on her face
what I later learn is ecstasy,
o fontem aquae vivae.

'Incapable of sensation and beyond oneself'
like Theresa of Bernin,
like the gaze of certain victims of torture,

ou dans les yeux de ceux qui s'aiment quand
le plaisir prend la forme du tourment.
L'extase, donc. L'extase pure et nue.

Les bras retombent, les lèvres ne happent
plus que le vide, le souffle se meurt.

Si l'âme existe, c'est alors qu'elle s'échappe
du corps sans gloire de Clémence, la servante du Seigneur.

or in the eyes of lovers when
pleasure turns to torment.
Ecstasy then. Ecstasy pure and simple.

Her arms drop down, her lips catch
nothing save the void, breath dies.

If the soul exists, then this is the moment it flies from
the unglorious body of Clémence, the servant of the Lord.

TOMBEAU DE FRANÇOISE DELCARTE
(1936-1996)

Notre biographie s'est arrêtée très tôt
Quelque chose n'aura pas été écrit
(F.D.)

Eteints le bruit et la fureur, éteint
le feu des grands discours incendiaires.
Celle qui traversa nos jours
comme un courant parcourt la mer
changeant la couleur de ses eaux
transformant sa teneur en sel
modifiant sa chaleur solaire
celle qui n'a fait que passer
a rendu son âme épuisée

Dans cette franciscaine église
où derrière toi nous entrons,
le portrait du Pauvre d'Assise,
celui dont tu portais le nom.
Et pauvre aussi la faible flamme
du cierge unique devant quoi
ton corps dépouillé de son âme
attend dans son fourreau de bois

Il fut un arbre aux branches habitées
qui bourdonnait d'insectes et d'oiseaux
comme ton front bourdonnait de poèmes.
L'un fut livré aux scies, aux marteaux,
l'autre torturé par lui-même.

Arbre tout frissonnant de feuilles
sous lequel tu parlais d'amour
sans y voir l'ombre du cercueil
qu'il deviendrait peut-être un jour,

FRANÇOISE DELCARTE'S GRAVE
(1936-1996)

Our biography was over too soon
Something won't have been written
(F.D.)

Smother the noise and the rage, smother
the fire of those incendiary speeches.
She who swept through our days
like a current travelling the sea
changing the colour of its waters
transforming its salt content
modifying its solar heat
she who simply passed through
has surrendered her spent soul

In the Franciscan church
which we enter behind you,
the portrait of the Poor Man of Assisi,
he whose name you bore.
Poor too the feeble flame
of the single candle in front of which
your body stripped of its soul
waits in its wooden sheath

It was once a tree with inhabited branches
that hummed with insects and birds
the way your head hummed with poems.
One was surrendered to the hammer and saw,
the other tortured by itself.

Tree a-tremble with leaves
beneath which you talked of love
unaware of the shadow of the coffin
it might one day become,

arbre aux bourgeons gonflé de sève
dont frémissait chaque rameau
à present mort comme tes rêves,
aussi rigide que ta peau.

Les six planches de bois font leur office,
l'arbre, le corps, l'un portant l'autre, l'un
cachant ce qu'est devenu l'autre.

Que reste-t-il encor de toi ? Si peu.
Partie en d'autres temps, vers d'autres lieux
pour — enfin — retrouver ta vie.

Ta vie que tu jetais aux chiens
espérant qu'ils en rongent les déchets
que sous leurs dents n'en reste rien,
ta vie qui n'en finissait pas
de mourir, ta vie dérisoire.

La voix du prêtre, le fatras des lieux-communs
où quelquefois affleure une lueur,
où le chagrin se lénifie.

Le ciel était encore si limpide.
Tes jours te précédaient encore si nombreux
(pensions-nous). Tu les as jetés au feu,
un à la fois, puis de plus en plus vite.

Toutes les choses que tu n'as pas faites
Qui pourra les faire à ta place ? Qui
boira le vin de la vendange d'après toi ?

Quelque chose n'a pas été écrit.
Peut-être un jour le ferai-je à ta place.

tree with buds swollen with sap
whose every branch quivered
now dead like your dreams,
and as stiff as your skin.

The six planks of wood fulfil their purpose,
tree, body, each bears the other, the one
conceals what the other has become.

What's left of what was you? So little.
Gone to another time, another clime
in order to — at last — rediscover your life.

The life you threw to the dogs
in the hope they'd pick at the scraps
until nothing was left in their teeth,
the life that was forever
dying, your wretched life.

The voice of the priest, the muddle of the commonplace
where a light sometimes surfaces,
where sorrow is soothed.

The sky was still so clear.
The days ahead still so numerous
(we thought). You threw them into the fire,
one by one, then faster and faster.

All the things you never did
Who will be able to do them for you? Who
do you think will drink the wine of the harvest?

Something hasn't been written.
I might one day do it for you.

Moi seule ai su le nombre de tes plaies,
la profondeur des eaux où tu marchais,
la hauteur du ciel étoilé.

Nous tournons autour du cercueil
pour aller baiser la relique.

« Surtout ne pas suivre la route
entre les rails, surtout ne pas
marcher au pas docile des petits soldats ».

Pérorant au long des soirées
ceux qui seraient les auteurs de demain
déconstruisaient le monde d'aujourd'hui
plus ivres de paroles que d'alcool.

Mais toi, tu y croyais.
Tu te grisais de l'un comme des autres.
Ils t'emportaient sur leurs ailes avant
de t'abandonner seule et pauvre
de te grignoter lentement.

Au son d'un harmonium acide les amis
Emboîtent le pas aux porteurs.
« In paradisum deducant te Angeli... »

Françoise, le soleil sur nos épaules.
Il ne brillait pas très souvent.
Je ne veux penser qu'à ces aubes
où le jour s'annonçait vivant.

Tu regardais la mer, tu espérais
arriver de l'autre côté,

I alone knew the number of your wounds,
the depth of the waters you trod,
the height of the starry sky.

We circle slowly about the coffin
in order to come and kiss the relic.

'Above all do not take the road
between the rails, above all do not
walk at the tame pace of the brave.'

Holding forth night after night
those who would be the authors of tomorrow
deconstructed the world of today
more drunk on words than alcohol.

But you, you believed in it.
You got as high on one as on the others.
They carried you away on their wings and then
abandoned you alone and poor
to gnaw slowly at yourself.

At the sound of an acid harmonium the friends
fall in behind the bearers.
'In paradisum deducant te Angeli...''
Françoise, the sun on our shoulders.
It didn't shine too often.
I want to think only of the dawns
of days that held the promise of life.

You watched the sea, you hoped
to reach the other side

mais tu ne savais pas nager.
Tu n'as jamais voulu apprendre.
Quelle importance. Où que tu sois
maintenant, au-delà des sables,
tu nous regardes, maladroits,
empêtrés de nos corps friables.

Quelque part, les patientes pluies
commencent à polir tes os

but you couldn't swim.
You never wanted to learn.
What does it matter. Wherever you are
now, beyond the sands,
you are watching us, awkward,
trapped in our friable bodies.

Somewhere, the patient rains
begin to polish your bones

GRISE BELGIQUE

« *Il n'y a pas de Belges* » dit au roi Albert
(premier du nom) ce bon Monsieur Destrée
qui n'avait pas souvent dedans la mer
trempé le fond de ses culottes d'écolier.
Aujourd'hui il verrait grâce à l'informatique
au mot belge répondre les entrées
qui rattachent quelqu'un à la Belgique.

N'en prenons qu'une, au bout de l'E quarante
(de tous nos chemins celui où l'on perd
le plus facilement patience quand le
vendredi soir on roule vers la mer.)

C'est là qu'on devient belge, là
qu'on va pêcher ses premières crevettes.
Venus de Zottengem ou de Waha,
c'est là que tous ensemble on fait trempette.

Que belges sommes dans notre âme
toute bercée au vent du Nord,
le regard plein des courtes lames
des flots farouches, et le corps
fouetté par la pluie inlassable,
belges depuis le premier sable
de la première plage, du
Zoute à La Panne, au temps perdu
bien perdu des jolies vacances
de notre belgicaine enfance.

Monsieur Destrée sans doute n'a jamais
mangé de gaufres chez Siska ni vu la sûre
montée des eaux vers son château de sable. Mais
il a créé, pour la littérature,

94

GREY BELGIUM

'There's no such thing as a Belgian,' King Albert was told
(the first of that name) by the worthy Mister Destrée
who had rarely dipped into the sea
the seat of his schoolboy pants.
Today with the help of IT he'd see
in response to the word Belgian, entries
that link a person to Belgium.

Let us take just one, at the end of the E40
(of all our roads this is the one that
so easily has us lose patience when on
Friday evenings we drive to the coast.)

That is where we become Belgian, where
we net our first shrimps.
Venus of Zottegem or Waha,
that is where together we go for a dip.

Belgians we are in our souls
rocking to the North wind,
eyes filled with the stunted breakers
of the bashful swell, bodies
lashed by the unrelenting rain,
Belgians since the first sand
of the first beach, from Le
Zoute to La Panne, in the past
very distant past of the lovely holidays
of our Belgican childhood.

Mister Destrée probably never
ate waffles at Siska's nor marked the water's
steady progress towards his sandcastle. But
he founded, for literature,

l'A-CA-DÉ-MIE. En être vous permet
de fréquenter aimable compagnie
et de garer sans problème votre voiture
entre Palais et Porte de Namur.

Mais quand son buste je contemple
un peu tragédien, un peu clerc,
je comprends bien qu'avec cette ample
toison, il n'y voyait pas clair.

Ecarte ces mèches ô Jules,
il y a des Belges partout,
natifs de Rabat, d'Istambule,
de Palerme, de Tombouctou.

Mais aussi des bords de la Meuse,
de son cousin proche, l'Escaut,
tu verras venir les fameuses
tribus échappées au tombeau.

Les anciens, sapés dans leurs braies,
Les nouveaux, moulés dans leurs jeans.
En voilà, des Belges, Destrée,
il en pleut, de tout origine.

Lorsque je me promène dans Bruxelles
j'entends parler tous les belges sabirs
(plus quelques autres). Dans l'universelle
chaleur humaine je suis prise, je respire
cet air bien de chez nous, cet air de bon aloi,
qui nous fait préférer, on ne sait trop pourquoi,
aux Iles sous le vent, notre plaine bourrue
et les pâteux accents qui traînent dans ses rues.

the A-CA-DE-MY. To belong gives one
the right to pleasant company
and trouble-free parking
between Palais and Porte de Namur.

But when I study his bust,
part tragic actor, part clerk,
I can understand why, with his great
mane of hair, he couldn't see too clearly.

O Jules, brush aside those locks,
there are Belgians everywhere,
natives of Rabat and Istanbul,
of Palermo and Timbuktu.

Furthermore, from the banks of the Meuse
and its near relation the Escaut,
you can see arriving the famous
tribes that have fled the grave.

Ancient ones, dressed in breeches,
Modern ones, moulded in jeans.
Well, there you have it, Destrée,
it's raining Belgians, all manner of Belgians.

Whenever I wander round Brussels
I hear all the Belgian lingoes spoken
(plus a few others). In the universal
human heat I am held, I breathe
the air that is so much ours, the fine air
that makes us prefer, though we couldn't say why,
our rugged plain to the windy Isles,
and the thick accents that linger in the streets.

Cet air, son souvenir me prend aux tripes quand,
à des milliers de bornes, dans la chaleur triste,
je revois tel café de Namur ou de Gand
où l'on sert au tonneau une brune trappiste
Cet air qui ne vaut rien m'est plus cher que les autres.
Plus que celui, paradisiaque, au grand soleil,
des sables bétonnés où le peuple se vautre,
c'est notre air sous la pluie, il n'a pas son pareil.

Grise la mer et grises les façades,
grise l'humeur, gris le ciel et le temps.
Sur tout le gris de ce pays, le fade
petit bonheur de ces petites gens.
Gris les reflets dans les canaux qui traînent,
gris les nuages sur les hauts-plateaux,
gris l'horizon bouché, grise la plaine,
gris le brouillard à couper au couteau.

Grises les routes qui serpentent
sous l'uniforme ciel de plomb
et grises les rivières lentes,
entre les perches de houblon,
gris les lointains salis de brume,
les prés malades gorgés d'eau,
les étroits jardins de légumes
et les champs tirés au cordeau,
gris les villages qui bossuent
le paysage, les maisons
fières de se montrer cossues
avec leurs nains sur le gazon.

A vingt ans j'écoutais passer les trains,
ventre noué, si forte était l'envie
de m'en aller vers ces pays lointains

This air, the thought of it wrenches my guts when,
thousands of miles away in the cheerless heat,
I picture a particular café in Namur or Ghent
where Trappist beer is served from the barrel.
This air, worth nothing, is dearer to me than any other.
Dearer than the heavenly air in the hot sun
of the concrete sands where the masses sprawl,
it's our air in the rain, there is nothing like it.

Grey the sea and grey the facades,
grey the mood, grey the sky and the weather.
Above all the grey of the country, the dull
little pleasures of the ordinary people.
Grey the reflections in the canals that linger,
grey the clouds on the high plateaux,
grey the overcast horizon, grey the plain,
grey the fog you could cut with a knife.

Grey the roads that snake
beneath a uniform leaden sky
and grey the slow rivers
between the hop-poles,
grey the distance sullied with mist,
the sick waterlogged meadows,
the narrow vegetable gardens
and dead straight fields,
grey the villages that hunch
the landscape, houses
proud to look stylish
with their gnomes on the lawn,

Aged twenty I'd listen to the trains go by,
stomach in a knot, so strong was my yearning
to visit the distant lands

appris aux leçons de géographie.
Maldives, Lofoten, Désolation
et « Sainte Hélène, petite isle »
comme un jour ''écrivit Napoléon
dans un cahier, en son temps juvénile.

Notre destin quelquefois nous précède.
Je n'ai jamais repéré Charleroi,
dans mon atlas. La ville la plus laide
est pourtant celle où je me sens chez moi.

Dans ce terreau où fut la houille,
où tant de mineurs ont souffert,
où sera bientôt ma dépouille
programmée au festin des vers.

Où personne de mon lignage,
n'a dormi. (Car sur ces lopins
cadastrés, au bout du voyage,
on ne choisit pas ses voisins).

Artisans, épiciers, notaires,
chiens de race ou bâtards perdus,
nous voilà dans la même terre,
dans le même trou confondus.

Flamands ou Wallons. Lorsque l'herbe
nous chatouille entre les orteils
on perd son parler, sa superbe,
on se trouve à chacun pareil.

Pas si loin de Monsieur Destrée.
dans le sol carolorégien

I'd studied in geography.
The Maldives, Lofoten, Desolation
and 'Saint Helena, a small island,'
as Napoleon one day wrote
in a notebook in his youth.

Fate sometimes precedes us.
I never found Charleroi
in my atlas. Yet this ugliest of towns
is where I feel at home.

In the compost where coal used to be,
where so many miners suffered,
where my mortal remains will soon
appear at the worms' feast.

Where none of my lineage
has slept. (For in these registered
plots, at the end of the journey,
we do not choose our neighbours).

Artisans, grocers, lawyers,
pedigree dogs and stray mongrels,
we lie in the same earth,
commingle in the same hole.

Flemish or Walloon. When the grass
tickles between our toes and our
power of speech and disdain is gone,
we discover we are the same.

Not that far from Mister Destrée
in the soil of the Charleroi area

101

lorsque je serai enterrée
que j'aurai défait tous mes liens

qui donc me tiendra compagnie
pour voir qu'il n'y a rien à voir ?
Qui, dedans la nuit infinie,
près de moi aura peur du noir ?

in the soil of the Charleroi area
when I have been buried
when I have loosed all ties

who then will keep me company
and see there is nothing to see?
Who, in the everlasting night,
at my side will fear the dark?

The Dedalus Press Poetry Europe Series:

1: **Sorgegondolen** : *The Sorrow Gondola*
Tomas Tranströmer : (Sweden) translated by *Robin Fulton*

2: **Dingfest** : *Thingsure*
Ernst Jandl : (Austria) translated by *Michael Hamburger*

3: **Aux Banquets du Diable** : *At the Devil's Banquets*
Anise Koltz : (Luxembourg) translated by *John F. Deane*

4: **L'Homme et ses Masques** : *Man and his Masks*
Jean Orizet : (France) translated by *Pat Boran*

5: **Libretto** : *Libretto*
Edoardo Sanguineti : (Italy) translated by *Pádraig J. Daly*

6: **Stances perdues** : *Lost Quatrains*
Alain Bosquet : (France) translated by *Roger Little*

7: **A Tenenat Here**: Selected Poems
Pentti Holappa : (Finland) translated by *Herbert Lomas*

8: **Ljus av ljus** : *Light From Light*
Ingemar Leckius : (Sweden) translated by *John F. Deane*

9: **Sommerfugledalen** : *Butterfly Valley*
Inger Christensen : (Denmark) translated by *Susanna Nied*

10. **Bercée au vent du Nord** : *Rocking to the North Wind*
Liliane Wouters : (Belgium) translated by *Anne-Marie Glasheen*